DATE DUE

The Torah contains sacred laws and texts

Hanukkah

Steve Potts

A⁺
Smart Apple Media

✡ Published by Smart Apple Media

1980 Lookout Drive, North Mankato, MN 56003

Designed by Rita Marshall

Copyright © 2002 Smart Apple Media. International copyright reserved in
all countries. No part of this book may be reproduced in any form without
written permission from the publisher.

Printed in the United States of America

✡ Photographs by Archive Photos, Bob Ecker, Beryl Goldberg, Sonia
Halliday, Terrance Klassen, Richard Nowitz, P.C. Robinson

✡ Library of Congress Cataloging-in-Publication Data

Potts, Steve. Hanukkah / by Steve Potts. p. cm. — (Holidays series)

Includes index.

✡ ISBN 1-58340-116-4

1. Hanukkah—Juvenile literature. 2. Hanukkah. [1. Holidays.] I. Title.

BM695.H3.P68 2001   296.4'35—dc21   00-067908

✡ First Edition 9 8 7 6 5 4 3 2 1

Hanukkah

CONTENTS

Miracle of Hanukkah

One of the many holidays celebrated by Jewish people is Hanukkah, which can also be spelled this way: Chanukah. This Jewish holiday is celebrated for eight days in November or December. It is one of the world's oldest holidays. ✡ In 168 B.C., the Jews of Judea—now Israel—had been conquered by the Greek-Syrian king Antiochus IV. He tried to force the Jews to worship Greek gods instead of their one true God. Though outnumbered, the Jews rebelled, led by Mattathias the Hasmonean and later his son Judah the

Maccabee. ✡ After three years of fighting, the Maccabees

successfully chased the **pagans** out of the holy Temple on

Jerusalem's Mount Moriah. The Temple was then rededicated

Temple ruins on Mount Moriah

to God with a new altar. ✡ In honor of the victory, religious custom called for the Jews to burn oil for eight nights. Sadly, there was only enough oil to burn for one night. Then a miracle happened: the little bit of oil burned for eight nights!

The Eight-day Holiday

Hanukkah is the celebration of that miracle. Just as their ancestors celebrated for eight days when the altar in Jerusalem was dedicated, Jewish people today also celebrate for eight days. Many Jews call the holiday the Festival of Lights,

A model of an ancient Jewish synagogue

the Festival of Consecration, or the Feast of Dedication. The holiday's most common name, Hanukkah, comes from the Hebrew word for dedication. ✡ Hanukkah is celebrated during the month on the Jewish calendar called **Kislev**. The celebration begins on the 25th day of that month and lasts for eight days. Much celebration, gathering of friends and relatives, and prayer takes place during each of Hanukkah's eight days.

The Menorah

An important Hanukkah custom is the lighting of the **menorah**. This is a candle stand that holds nine candles.

There is one candle for each of the eight nights of Hanukkah

and a shorter candle that is called the shammus, or servant

candle. This candle is used to light the other eight. The first

A menorah shaped like a row of buildings

night of Hanukkah, a candle is put on the far right end of the menorah. The servant candle is lit and three prayers are said.

✡ The servant candle is used to light the first candle and is then put back in the menorah. The candles should burn for at least 30 minutes. Each night of Hanukkah, another candle is put in

The lighting of the menorah is known in Hebrew as the hanukiya.

the menorah and lit. The candles are put in the menorah from right to left, but they are lit from left to right. Prayers are offered for peace, strength, hope, and freedom. ✡ On the

During Hanukkah, some Jews read from the Torah

eighth night of Hanukkah, all of the candles are lit. People say prayers and sing songs. The candles slowly burn out. The menorah is put away until it is used again the next year.

Hanukkah Festivities

Today, Hanukkah is also celebrated by giving presents and eating special foods. Parents often give their children gifts of gelt (chocolate coins) or other small tokens. One traditional gift is the dreidel. This is a top that spins. In ancient Palestine, when the Syrians outlawed the reading of the

Wooden dreidels and a handful of gelt

Torah, people carried a dreidel with them so they could pretend to be playing with it if they were ever caught reading the Torah. ✡ While many Christians give gifts on Christmas Eve or Christmas Day, many Jewish people give gifts each day of Hanukkah—that's eight gifts! ✡ Hanukkah is also a time to feast on special foods. Many traditional Hanukkah foods are cooked in oil, in remembrance of the oil that burned in the Temple in Jerusalem. One food that came to North America from Eastern European Jews is latkes, or potato pancakes, which are often

The dreidel got its modern name from the German word for "top."

eaten with applesauce and sour cream. In Israel, the favorite

Hanukkah food is sufganiya, a kind of jelly donut cooked in

oil. Israeli Jews eat sufganiya for more than a month before the

Potato pancakes are fried in oil until crisp

start of Hanukkah. ✡ Eating cheese is another Hanukkah tradition. This is done in memory of Judith, a woman who saved her village from the Syrians by tricking the Syrian general Holofernes. She fed him wine and cheese until he fell asleep, and then she killed him. ✡ For Jewish people, Hanukkah **Judaism, the oldest living religion, claims more than 14 million believers worldwide.** is one of the most festive holidays of the year. The eight-day Festival of Lights brings Jewish families together around the world to celebrate their heritage and their faith.

A Jewish boy reading stories of his faith

Hanukkah Activity

Part of the Hanukkah celebration is sending and receiving decorative cards. This colorful card holder will make displaying Hanukkah cards fun and easy.

What You Need

20–30 wooden spring-type clothespins

Tempera paints (gold and blue Hanukkah colors)

Three yards (2.7 m) of gold, silver, or brightly colored cord

Hanukkah cards

Old newspapers

Paint brushes

A bowl of water

What You Do

Cover your work space with the old newspapers. Paint both sides of the clothespins. When the clothespins are dry, thread the cord through the spring hole in each clothespin. Make sure all the clothespins are facing the same direction. Space them two to three inches (5–8 cm) apart. Then, hang your card holder on a mantel or over an inside doorway (use small finishing nails or push pins). Hang a Hanukkah card from each clothespin and enjoy!

A menorah in the shape of an artist's palette

INFORMATION

Index

Words to Know

Kislev—the third month in the Jewish calendar

menorah—a candleholder that holds nine candles; the menorah is used in the celebration of Hanukkah

pagans—people who do not believe in one true God, but who worship many gods or trust in magic

Palestine—the area of the Middle East currently called Israel and Jordan

Torah—the written history and laws of the Jewish religion

Read More

Berger, Gilda. *Celebrate! Stories of the Jewish Holidays*. New York: Scholastic Press, 1998.

Fischer, Sara, and Barbara Klebanow. *American Holidays: Exploring Traditions, Customs, and Backgrounds*. Brattleboro, Vt.: Pro Lingua Associates, 1986.

Kindersley, Anabel. *Celebrations*. New York: DK Publishing, 1997.

Ziefert, Harriet. *Eight Days of Hanukkah: A Holiday Step Book*. New York: Viking Books, 1997.

Internet Sites

Chanukah on the Net

http://www.holidays.net/chanukah/index.htm

AICE-JSOURCE

http://www.us-israel.org/jsource/Judaism/holiday7.html